John Harrold '94.

CONTENTS

RUPERT AND THE SPACESHIP 6

RUPERT AND THE PEACOCK HEDGE 23

RUPERT AND THE BEACHCOMBERS 40

RUPERT AND THE QUEEN'S VISIT 57

RUPERT AND UNCLE BORIS 74

ACTIVITY PAGES

A Page to Colour 33
Spot the Difference 83
Answers to Puzzle 93

STORIES BY IAN ROBINSON

ILLUSTRATED BY JOHN HARROLD

STORY COLOURING BY GINA HART AND DORIS CAMPBELL

© Express Newspapers plc 1994

This book belongs to:

....

John Harrold.

RUPERT

THE DAILY EXPRESS ANNUAL

John Harrold.

Pedigree
BOOKS

No 59

Published by Pedigree Books Limited, The Old Rectory, Matford Lane, Exeter, EX2 4PS

RUPERT and

One evening, Rupert's puzzled by
A bright light glowing in the sky.

One evening, Rupert is getting ready for bed when he suddenly notices a strange light, low in the sky. At first he thinks it must be a star, but, as he looks more closely, he sees it glide slowly across Nutwood Common, lighting up the trees and grass as it goes by. "Look outside!" he calls to his mother, but by the time Mrs. Bear comes to the window there is nothing to be seen. "How odd!" says Rupert. "I wonder what it was?"

the Spaceship

*"Look, Mum!" he calls, but Mrs. Bear
Peers out to find there's nothing there!*

*Next day his father says they've found
A strange new circle on the ground . . .*

Next morning, Rupert's father reads a strange story from the newspaper. "They've found a big circle of flattened grass up on the common," he declares. "The reporter thinks it might have been made by a spaceship . . ." "Goodness!" gasps Mrs. Bear. "Don't worry!" he chuckles. "I expect the grass has just been crushed by a strong gust of wind. "I wonder?" thinks Rupert, remembering the light he saw last night . . .

*"A spaceship!" Rupert thinks. "I'm sure
That must explain the light I saw!"*

RUPERT HELPS GREGORY SEARCH

He hurries out to where the light
He saw was moving, late last night.

It seems there's nothing there to see,
Except Rupert's pal, Gregory . . .

He's looking for a spaceship too
"I saw the same bright light as you!"

Then, as the pair search, Rupert sees
A strange mark near a stand of trees . . .

As soon as breakfast is over, Rupert decides to go and investigate the strange circle. He sets off across the common but can see no sign of anything out of the ordinary. As he looks all round, he spots his pal Gregory Guinea-pig, who also seems to be searching the common. "I wonder if he's found anything?" thinks Rupert. "Hello!" he calls. "Wait for me . . ." Gregory looks up with a start, then waves back as Rupert hurries over to join him.

"Hello!" cries Gregory. "I suppose you've come to look for the spaceship?" "Yes," says Rupert. "I saw a strange light in the sky last night and thought . . ." "I saw it too!" squeaks Gregory. "One minute it was hovering over the common, then it suddenly disappeared! I'm sure it *must* have been a spaceship, but I haven't found anything yet!" "Neither have I!" admits Rupert. Just then he spots a strange mark on the ground by the edge of the woods . . .

RUPERT FINDS THE CIRCLE

"Gosh!" Rupert cries. "Just look at that!
A circle of grass, squashed down flat . . ."

"The spaceship landed here and then
Took off into the sky again."

The two friends hear a rustling sound
"Who's there?" calls Rupert, turning round . . .

A terrifying spaceman comes
With heavy tread towards the chums!

As the two pals hurry towards the edge of the woods, they see the grass has been crushed flat in a huge circle . . . "It's enormous!" cries Rupert. "Do you think it's *really* where a spaceship landed?" marvels Gregory. "I don't know," says Rupert. "My father thought it might have been caused by a gust of wind . . ." "What a pity it didn't stay longer," sighs Gregory, still thinking of the spaceship. "I wonder what it looked like?"

Gregory is still looking wistfully at the strange circle when Rupert hears a rustling sound. "What was that?" asks Gregory, nervously. "I don't know," whispers Rupert. The pals are sure they can hear someone crashing through the undergrowth. "Who's there?" calls Rupert. Nobody answers, but the next moment the pair see a sinister figure advancing towards them. "Help!" cries Gregory. "It's a spaceman!"

END OF PART 1

9

RUPERT
and the Spaceship

A second spaceman comes in sight
As Gregory runs off in fright.

"We'll conquer you!" the spacemen call
But then one trips and starts to fall . . .

The other spaceman trips as well
And tumbles with a sudden yell.

His helmet flies off. It's a box –
The masked invader's Freddy Fox!

As Gregory flees into the woods, a second spaceman lurches out after the first. "Greetings, Earthling!" it booms. "We have travelled far to reach your planet . . ." "W . . . who are you?" gasps Rupert. "Galactic invaders!" cry the spacemen. "We have come to conquer the whole of Nutwood . . ." Rupert doesn't wait to hear any more, but turns to run away. "Stop!" cry the spacemen, lumbering after him, then one of them stumbles and starts to topple over . . .

To Rupert's surprise the second spaceman doesn't seem to notice his companion lying sprawled on the ground. "Oh, no!" he wails as he trips over and lands in a heap at Rupert's feet. "Freddy Fox!" he cries as the 'Galactic invader's' helmet comes flying off. "Er, hello, Rupert," groans Freddy. "Give me a hand up, could you? It's jolly difficult to move in these cardboard suits . . ." "It's hard to breathe too!" groans Ferdy from the bottom of the pile.

10

RUPERT UNCOVERS A HOAX

"It's such a shame our joke went wrong,
You were the first to come along!"

"We crushed the grass, then lay in wait
To see who would investigate."

"It worked!" laughs Rupert. "Now help me
To find where Gregory can be . . ."

The guinea-pig soon hears them call,
"I've found the spaceship after all!"

"You're not cross, are you?" says Freddy. "We didn't mean any harm. It was only a practical joke . . ." "A good one!" laughs Rupert. "For a moment there, I thought you really *were* visitors from Outer Space!" The Foxes explain that they made the circle late one evening, when nobody was about. "We never dreamt it would get into the papers!" says Freddy. "But then we decided to dress up as the spacemen and play a trick on the first people to come along."

"No hard feelings!" Rupert tells the Foxes. "But I really ought to go and tell poor Gregory that everything's all right. You really gave him quite a fright . . ." "We'll help you look," says Ferdy. "I expect he's still hiding somewhere in the woods . . ." The three pals set out together, but haven't gone far before they see the little guinea-pig, running towards them, smiling delightedly! "Hello!" he calls. "I think I've found the spacemen's flying saucer! Come and see . . ."

RUPERT'S PAL FINDS A SPACESHIP

"There isn't one!" the chums declare,
But Gregory insists it's there . . .

"I know it's small, but, even so,
I've found the Nutwood U.F.O."

"A toy!" the Foxes laugh, then see
How heavy the small craft must be!

The spaceship Gregory has found
Begins to make a humming sound . . .

"The spaceship's in a clearing behind these trees!" explains Gregory, excitedly. "But there *weren't* any spacemen!" says Rupert. "It was only the Foxes pretending!" "Not *them*!" insists Gregory. "They're far too big. It's a different spaceship I'm talking about. I found it when I was looking for somewhere to hide . . ." Following Gregory into the woods, Rupert is amazed to see a tiny flying saucer. "There!" says Gregory . "What do you make of that?"

To Gregory's annoyance the two Foxes burst out laughing at the sight of the flying saucer. "Good try!" chuckles Freddy. "But you can't expect us to believe that's a real spaceship! Anyone can see it's only a toy . . ." "You don't understand!" says Gregory. "I know it *looks* like a toy, but it's far too heavy to lift." "He's right!" gasps Rupert. All of a sudden the chums hear a strange humming sound as a light on the top of the spaceship begins to glow . . .

RUPERT AND HIS CHUMS SHRINK

A periscope begins to swing
To where the pals stand marvelling . . .

Next moment there's a dazzling light
Which blinds the chums – it seems so bright!

Then, as it fades, they're shocked to see
The ship start growing rapidly . . .

*"It **looks** much bigger now, but all*
That's happened is that we've grown small!"

"I wonder what's happening?" says Rupert. To his surprise, the glowing light rises up, like a periscope, then swivels round towards the astonished chums. "I don't like the look of this!" mutters Ferdy. "Perhaps Gregory's right. It might be real after all . . ." The next moment, the whole clearing is suddenly flooded with a brilliant purple light. "I c . . . can't move!" squeaks Gregory. "Neither can I!" gasps Rupert, screwing up his eyes against the dazzling glare.

The purple light soon starts to fade and the pals are astonished to see the tiny spaceship looming up in front of them. "It's growing bigger!" cries Gregory. "You're right!" marvels Ferdy, rubbing his eyes in disbelief. It's only as the chums turn to look at the rest of the clearing that they realise what's *really* happened . . . "The spaceship hasn't grown at all!" gasps Rupert. "*We've* been shrinking smaller and smaller. Look at that fir-cone and the height of the grass . . ."

RUPERT SEES THE SPACEMEN

Before the pals can move, a door
Swings open. "Now what lies in store?"

Two figures suddenly appear,
*"**Real** spacemen!" Ferdy gasps in fear.*

"Look!" Freddy cries. "Another one!
They've come to catch us! Quick, let's run!"

Then Rupert says the pals all should
Find hiding places in the wood . . .

When the pals stop shrinking, the spaceship seems vast. "It must have come from Outer Space!" gasps Freddy. "But why did they bother to shrink us with that purple ray?" Before anyone can answer, there is a sudden whirring sound from inside the ship and a door starts to swing open. At first nothing happens, then Rupert sees a pair of shadowy figures moving at the top of the ramp. "Real spacemen!" cries Gregory. "They don't look very friendly!" gulps Ferdy.

A third figure appears in the doorway of the spaceship as the first two lurch down the ramp towards the pals. "Come on!" cries Freddy. "Let's make a run for it. They're going to catch us and take us back to their planet . . ." The chums are so small that the grass seems like a forest, with flowers and bushes towering above them like trees. "We'll never get away from them like this," says Rupert. "Let's make for the woods, where there'll be somewhere to hide . . ."

RUPERT'S PALS ARE CAPTURED

"This way!" he calls. "All follow me!
We'll hide inside this hollow tree . . ."

But Gregory trips over and
Ferdy stops to lend him a hand.

Rupert and Freddy watch as they
Are caught and briskly marched away!

They've got to save the pair, but how
Can Rupert stop the spacemen now?

By the edge of the forest, Rupert spots a hole at the foot of a hollow tree. "We should be safe in here!" he calls. As the others follow him, Gregory trips on a stone and goes flying through the air. Ferdy sees what's happened and stops to help him to his feet. "Come on!" he urges. "They can't be far behind . . ." As Gregory picks himself up the three spacesmen come running through the grass towards them. "Oh, no!" groans Rupert. "They're bound to be caught!"

Rupert and Freddy look on helplessly from their hiding place, as the spacemen capture their pals. "Let us go!" protests Ferdy, but the spacemen ignore his cry and march briskly away with their prisoners. "They're taking them back to the ship!" whispers Freddy. "Yes," says Rupert. "Unless we do something, we might never see Ferdy or Gregory ever again!" "But what if *we* get caught too?" asks Freddy.

END OF PART 2

RUPERT
and the Spaceship

The pals creep back to where they saw
The spaceship. "There's an open door!"

No-one's about, so they decide
To risk a closer look, inside . . .

The ship's door closes with a click.
"Oh no!" groans Freddy. "It's a trick!"

"Look!" Rupert whispers. "I can see
The spacemen, there with Gregory . . ."

Being careful to keep well out of sight, Rupert and Freddy follow the spacemen back through the long grass. When they reach the spaceship, there is nobody to be seen. "They must have all gone inside!" whispers Rupert. The pair tip-toe cautiously towards the ramp but no one seems to have noticed them . . . "Let's risk a peep inside," says Rupert. "We might spot where the others are being held prisoner." "All right," agrees Freddy. "But don't make a sound!"

No sooner have Rupert and Freddy stepped inside the spaceship than the ramp swings up behind them. "It's a trick!" cries Freddy. "*We've* been captured too!" Looking up, the pair see Ferdy and Gregory, standing on an upper deck, while the spacemen are huddled over the ship's controls. "Quick, you two. Over here!" hisses Rupert. "Freddy and I have come to help . . ." "I do hope so!" says one of the spacemen, swinging round to face the startled newcomers . . .

16

RUPERT GETS A SURPRISE

*Their captain smiles. "Hello, you two!
I'm sorry if we frightened you . . ."*

*"There's really no need for alarm,
Your friends are safe. We mean no harm."*

*"We had a longer journey planned,
But freak storms meant we had to land . . ."*

*"The compass that we use to steer
Is broken, so we're stranded here!"*

To Rupert's surprise, the spacemen seem friendly . . . "Welcome aboard!" smiles their leader. "I'm sorry if we frightened you with our shrinking ray, but everything's so big here that we thought you might be dangerous!" "Us!" gasps Freddy. "But you're the ones who captured our chums . . ." "Don't worry," says Gregory. "They only wanted to find out where they'd landed." "You mean they don't know?" asks Rupert. "No!" says the spaceman.

"We only landed here by accident," explains the captain of the spaceship. "We come from a far-off planet, where everything is tiny and the people of your world would seem like giants. We were travelling through space one day when we flew into a celestial storm which blew us off course and damaged our ship's controls." "Yours was the first planet we came to," adds a second spaceman. "We can't go home until we've mended our galactic compass."

RUPERT HAS AN IDEA

*"If only we knew someone who
Could help to put it right, do you?"*

*"The old Professor! He might know!
That's where the spacemen ought to go!"*

*The spaceship's crew decide that they
Will fly to see him straightaway . . .*

*Poor Bodkin can't believe his eyes –
"A spaceship, whizzing through the skies!"*

"I tried to explain that we don't have spaceships in Nutwood!" explains Gregory. "But they didn't seem to understand." "I wonder what we can do to help?" says Rupert. He thinks hard for a moment, then gives a sudden cry. "Of course!" he smiles. "Nutwood may not have any spaceships, but there *is* someone here who knows all about flying machines . . ." "The Old Professor!" says Freddy. "I wonder what he'll make of a *real* flying saucer?"

When Rupert explains that the Professor's tower isn't far away, the captain is keen to fly there straight away. "It's only our compass that's damaged," he declares. "You can guide us, Rupert, while I steer the ship . . ." The pals peer out of the windows excitedly as the spaceship takes off. Soon they can see the top of the Professor's tower, and spot his servant, Bodkin, standing by the flagpole. He blinks in amazement, the, quickly hurries inside.

RUPERT FLIES IN A SPACESHIP

Then, through a window, open wide
The little spaceship flies inside . . .

The Professor's amazed to see
Who's there. "It's Rupert! Goodness me!"

He needs a lens to help him view
The spaceship and its tiny crew . . .

"I'd like to help you, but I think
*That first you'll have to make **me** shrink!"*

Rather than land on top of the tower, the spaceship swoops down and flies in through the open window of the Professor's study. "Good gracious!" he cries as it lands on his desk. "How extraordinary!" He is even more astonished when the door of the spaceship swings open and a little figure wearing a red jersey comes running out . . . "Hello Professor!" cries Rupert. "It's me!" "Rupert?" he gasps. "But you're tiny! Whatever's happened? And *whose* is this flying saucer?"

As Rupert starts to explain what's happened, Bodkin hurries into the room. "There's a *spaceship!*" he gasps, then breaks off as he sees the row of tiny figures on the Professor's desk. "Delighted to meet you!" the Professor tells the ship's captain, peering through a large magnifying glass . . . "I'd be happy to help, but I think you'll have to shrink me too. It's the only way I can get inside your spaceship and have a look at the controls . . ."

RUPERT'S FRIEND SAVES THE DAY

As soon as he's all set to go
The room fills with a purple glow . . .

With Bodkin's help, he joins the men
Who lead the way inside again.

It doesn't take him very long
To sort out what's been going wrong.

"Our spaceship's mended, thanks to you
Professor, and to Rupert too . . ."

Hurrying to collect a tool-kit from his work-shop, the Professor returns to the study and tells the spacemen to switch on their shrinking ray. The room is filled with a bright purple glow and an astonished Bodkin sees his master grow smaller and smaller . . . "Fascinating!" marvels the Professor as Bodkin picks him up and puts him on the desk. "This is all very exciting! I've never been inside a spaceship before." "This way," says the captain. "Follow me . . ."

As soon as they are inside the spaceship, the Professor takes out his screwdriver and begins to adjust the compass. "Nothing too serious!" he announces cheerfully. "That storm you encountered must have given it a bit of a knock." After a few moment's tinkering, he declares the compass mended. "Wonderful!" says the captain. "We'd never have managed it without your help." "A pleasure!" smiles the Professor. "But it's Rupert you should really thank."

RUPERT SAYS GOODBYE

A green light glows this time and all
The chums can feel themselves grow tall . . .

They look around and realise
They've all returned to normal size!

"Farewell!" the captain cries. "Now we
Must go back to our galaxy . . ."

The spaceship starts to hum and then
Flies through the window once again.

Now that the compass has been repaired, it only remains to turn all the Nutwooders back to their proper size. The lamp from the spaceship glows with a green light this time and, sure enough, Rupert can feel himself growing taller and taller . . . "Goodness!" laughs the Professor as they balance together on top of his desk. "There isn't much room up here, now that we're back to normal . . ." "Bravo!" cries Bodkin. "I was worried it wouldn't work!"

"Time for us to leave now!" the spaceship's captain tells Rupert. "We've got a long way to travel before we reach our home." "I'm glad you landed in Nutwood!" says Rupert. "I've always wanted to meet a visitor from Outer Space . . ." "Me too!" nods Freddy. "Playing at spacemen isn't nearly so exciting as flying in a *real* spaceship!" The door of the spaceship swings shut, its engines start to hum, then it rises up and speeds off out of the open window.

RUPERT KEEPS A SECRET

The chums all wave goodbye as they
Watch their new friends speed on their way.

"What an adventure this has been!
I can't believe the things we've seen!"

That evening, Mr. Bear reads how
The hoax has been uncovered now.

"If only he knew!" Rupert thinks.
He smiles at Gregory and winks . . .

From the top of the tower, Rupert and his pals can see the spaceship soaring high into the sky as it flies off over Nutwood. "Remarkable!" cries the Professor, peering through a telescope. "It's astonishing how quickly they can travel!" When the spaceship has finally disappeared from sight, the chums set off home, while the Professor decides to write a letter about their encounter to a learned magazine. "They'll never believe me!" he chuckles.

When Rupert arrives home for tea, he finds his father reading the paper . . . "That strange circle on the common has been revealed as a hoax!" he declares. "Somebody flattened the grass . . ." "It was a jolly clever joke!" says Rupert. "I suppose so," agrees Mr. Bear. "Except everyone knows there's no such thing as flying saucers . . ." "I wouldn't be too sure about that!" smiles Rupert, winking at Gregory . . .

THE END

RUPERT

and the

Peacock

Hedge

John Harrold.

RUPERT HELPS TO MAKE A PEACOCK

One fine day Mr. Bear says he
Will try his hand at topiary . . .

"We'll trim this hedge until we make
A peacock!" he says. "You can rake."

Eventually a bird appears –
"A perfect peacock!" Rupert cheers.

Then Mrs. Bear comes out to say
She hopes it doesn't fly away . . .

Mr. Bear has decided it's time to tidy up the garden ready for Spring. This year, he tells Rupert, he's going to try something special when it comes to trimming the hedge . . . "Will it *really* look like a peacock?" asks Rupert. "I hope so," smiles his father. "Let's see what we can do . . ." Climbing up to reach the top of the hedge he clips away with the shears until a large, green bird begins to take shape. "This is fun!" laughs Rupert, as he rakes up the cuttings.

After a lot of careful clipping, Mr. Bear finally announces that the Peacock Hedge is finished. "It's marvellous!" cries Rupert, and hurries inside to fetch his mother. "My goodness!" she says, when she sees what the pair have done. "I thought you were busy, but I had no idea you were up to something like this! It looks so lifelike. If I didn't know better, I'd say it was about to fly away . . ." "I hope not!" smiles Mr. Bear. After all that work I want to enjoy looking at it!"

RUPERT SEES SOME MAGIC

*When Tigerlily hears, she tells
How you can shape a hedge with spells.*

*"I've often seen my father trim
This lion hedge – let's start with him!"*

*The pals are all amazed to see
The hedge grow bigger instantly . . .*

*Another spell and back it shrinks –
"I don't believe it!" Podgy blinks.*

Next day, Rupert visits Tigerlily's house, together with Bill, Podgy and Ottoline. He tells them all about the Peacock Hedge and how his father spent all day trimming it into shape. "In our garden we have hedges like dragons and lions," says Tigerlily. "My father keeps them tidy with his magic wand . . ." "How?" asks Rupert. "Come and see," says Tigerlily, leading the way outside, to a fine green lion. "Watch carefully," she says, then points at it with her wand . . .

At first nothing happens, then the lion begins to grow bigger and bigger . . . "Gosh!" gasps Rupert as it towers over the startled chums. "Now for a spot of pruning!" laughs Tigerlily and waves the wand again. All at once, the hedge stops growing and begins to shrink back to its normal size . . . "Amazing!" blinks Podgy. "It's certainly easier than using shears!" chuckles Tigerlily. "Now let's all go to Rupert's garden. I want to see this peacock for myself . . ."

RUPERT'S CHUM CASTS A SPELL

At Rupert's house, the chums agree
The peacock's worked out splendidly.

But Tigerlily thinks a spell
Will help improve the bird as well . . .

When nothing happens everyone
Asks Tigerlily what she's done.

"You'll see!" she smiles. And so it proves,
For suddenly, the peacock moves!

When the chums arrive at Rupert's house, they all hurry into the garden to see the hedge. "You were right!" cries Bill. "It's even better than I'd imagined . . ." "Perfect!" says Podgy. "I saw a peacock at the zoo last summer . . ." "It's certainly very fine," agrees Tigerlily thoughtfully. "But I wonder if it could look even more lifelike?" Raising her wand, she points it at the peacock and starts to chant another spell. "Oh, no!" groans Rupert. "What now?"

To Rupert's relief, the peacock seems unaltered by Tigerlily's spell. "It can't have worked," says Ottoline. "Last time the hedge started growing straightaway . . ." "I wasn't trying to make it grow," says Tigerlily. "I wanted . . ." she breaks off as the pals hear a sudden rustle of leaves. "It moved!" cries Rupert as the peacock peers down at the astonished chums. "I don't believe it!" gasps Ottoline as the bird gives a loud cluck, and starts to preen its wing . . .

RUPERT CHASES THE PEACOCK

The peacock gives a raucous cry
Then flaps its wings and tries to fly . . .

"Oh, no!" cries Rupert in dismay –
The bird takes off and flies away!

Outside, Rupert's amazed to see
The peacock perching in a tree.

He clambers to the top but then
The bird squawks and flies off again!

"Now your hedge looks even more lifelike!" laughs Tigerlily as the peacock turns its head to look at the chums. She is so pleased with her joke that she doesn't notice the bird has lowered its tail and started to flap its wings. All of a sudden, it gives a loud squawk and takes off. "It's flying away!" cries Rupert. "That's not meant to happen!" gasps Tigerlily as the peacock clears the garden hedge and disappears from sight. "Come on!" calls Rupert. "Let's follow it . . ."

Running out of the garden, Rupert soon spots the peacock, perched on a high branch of a nearby tree. "Try calling to it," suggests Ottoline, but the bird shows no sign of wanting to come down. "There's only one thing for it!" declares Rupert and starts to climb the tree. At first the peacock seems curious but as Rupert gets closer, the bird gives a cry of alarm and flies off before he can reach it. "Oh, no!" he groans.

END OF PART 1

27

RUPERT
and the Peacock Hedge

It flies to Nutwood High Street where
The morning shoppers gasp and stare . . .

Mr. Anteater cries, "Bless me!
Is that a peacock hedge I see?"

The strange bird squawks – then on it speeds
While Rupert follows where it leads . . .

It lands upon a blind at last,
As P.C. Growler wanders past.

By the time Rupert has clambered down, the peacock has flown off towards the middle of Nutwood. How everyone stares to see the strange green bird flapping its way down the High Street! Mrs. Sheep gives a cry of alarm as it swishes over her head, while Mr. Anteater drops his cane and reels back in astonishment. "That peacock's feathers look just like leaves!" "They do a bit!" says Rupert. "Can't stop, I'm afraid, I've got to keep up to see where it lands . . ."

Hurrying down the High Street, Rupert catches up with the others just as the peacock passes the fishmonger's. "Good gracious!" gasps Mrs. Pug, "I don't believe it!" "Nor do I!" blinks the shopkeeper. Eventually the flyaway bird lands on a blind outside Mr. Chimp's shop. As the pals draw near, they see P.C. Growler approaching. "What's all this?" demands the policeman. "It looks as if that bird's escaped from Nutchester Zoo!"

RUPERT ASKS FOR BREADCRUMBS

*"That's odd!" he says. "This peacock's green!
It's not like other birds I've seen . . ."*

*He reaches out, but just before
The bird's caught it flies off once more . . .*

*"I know! You need to lay a trail
Of old breadcrumbs. They never fail!"*

*Rupert runs home to Mrs. Bear –
Is there some stale bread she can spare?*

"Wait a minute!" says Growler. "There's something very odd about this bird . . ." "It's a rare breed," explains Rupert hurriedly. "Quite different from any other peacock!" "I can see that," replies the policeman. "But what's it doing here in the middle of the High Street?" "It . . . it escaped," says Ottoline. "We tried to catch it, but it flew away . . ." "Leave this to me," says Growler and reaches up towards the bird. As he does so, it flaps its wings and takes to the air . . .

"Bother!" cries Growler as the bird flies out of sight. He thinks hard for a moment, then gives a sudden cry. "Breadcrumbs are what you need! My wife's always putting them out for the birds in our garden. If peacocks eat them too, then it's the perfect way to lure him back . . ." Rupert is delighted with his suggestion and hurries home to see if Mrs. Bear has any stale bread to spare. "Of course," she smiles. "I was saving some in case you wanted to feed the ducks."

RUPERT AND BILL CATCH THE BIRD

As soon as Rupert joins his chums
He starts to lay a trail of crumbs.

The peacock spots the bread and flies
To where the trail's beginning lies . . .

It starts to eat and Bill prepares
To catch the peacock unawares . . .

He grabs the bird, then cries "Hurray!
This time our friend won't get away!"

Running back to join the others, Rupert sets about laying a trail of breadcrumbs to entice the flyaway peacock. "That's the idea!" says Growler. "Just wait till it sees those . . ." "Let's lead it somewhere quieter," suggest Ottoline. "Good idea," agrees Rupert and continues the trail up on to the common. He has hardly finished scattering the last handful of crumbs when there is a raucous cry and the peacock comes swooping down towards the chums.

As soon as the peacock lands, it starts pecking eagerly at the breadcrumbs. "What now?" asks Ottoline. "It won't be long before they're all gone . . ." "I'll try to catch it off guard," declares Bill. Keeping well out of sight, he creeps round behind the bird, then inches slowly towards it. The moment he's close enough, he leaps forward and grabs the startled peacock before it can fly away. "Hurrah!" he cries triumphantly. "It won't escape so easily this time . . ."

RUPERT'S CHUM IS CARRIED OFF

The peacock calls out angrily
And struggles wildly to break free.

Then, suddenly, it tries to fly
And carries Bill up in the sky!

"We've got to rescue Bill, but how?"
It's up to Tigerlily now . . .

"Another spell might do the trick –
All back to the Pagoda, quick!"

As Bill holds on to the struggling peacock, his cry of triumph turns to one of alarm. "It's trying to break free!" he calls to the others. "Don't let go!" cries Rupert and hurries forward to help his friend. The bird starts to flap its wings frantically and squawks crossly, as if it's determined to get away. The next moment, it hops into the air and takes off, with an astonished Bill still hanging on as tightly as he can. "Stop!" calls Rupert when he sees what's happening, but it's too late . . .

The chums are all shocked by what has happened. "Come back!" gasps Ottoline as she watches Bill being carried off over the treetops. "We've got to rescue him!" declares Rupert. "Who knows where the peacock will fly to next?" "What can we do?" says Tigerlily. She thinks for a moment, then tells the others she's had an idea. "Follow me!" she calls, running back towards the Pagoda. "It was my magic that started all this, perhaps I can use it to help Bill . . .

She hurries home, then runs outside –
"We need a travel cloud to ride!"

"I'll conjure one up straightaway,
Please do exactly as I say . . ."

"To make a cloud, you need to pour
Ten drops from each flask in this drawer . . ."

The travel cloud spell soon begins –
"It's working!" Tigerlily grins.

When they reach the Pagoda, Tigerlily explains that her father has gone out for the morning, so she'll have to try another spell all by herself . . . She leads the way to a large metal bowl which stands glinting in the sunshine. "You and I must follow Bill," she tells Rupert. "A travel cloud will carry us across the skies . . ." "What's a travel cloud?" asks Podgy. "You'll see!" declares Tigerlily. "In fact, I need your help to make the spell work . . ."

The bowl is covered by a heavy grille, which Rupert and Tigerlily stand on while she tells Podgy what to do . . . Opening a little drawer, he takes out two bottles full of brightly coloured liquid. "They have to be mixed together," says Tigerlily. "If you pour ten drops from one bottle into the bowl, then Ottoline can measure out ten from the other . . ." Soon a thick mist starts to rise. "Good!" smiles Tigerlily. "The spell's working . . ."

END OF PART 2

32

See how carefully you can colour these two pictures of Rupert.

PART 3

RUPERT
and the Peacock Hedge

A thick white cloud engulfs the pair
And lifts them high into the air . . .

"The peacock!" Tigerlily cries –
"We'll follow everywhere it flies!"

Before long, they're surprised to find
The bird's left Nutwood far behind.

"Look!" Rupert cries. "I should have known!
The Bird King's castle's where it's flown!"

As Podgy and Ottoline look on in astonishment, the mist grows thicker, till it forms a cloud which carries Rupert and Tigerlily up into the sky. "Tell my father what's happened the moment he returns," she calls. "We'll be back as soon as we can . . ." Peering into the distance, Rupert spots the peacock, flying off with Bill. "After them!" commands Tigerlily and points at the bird with her wand. The cloud spins round, then starts to gather speed . . .

On and on the peacock flies, until all signs of Nutwood have been left far behind. "I wonder where it's going?" thinks Rupert. Suddenly, the bird starts to climb higher, up towards a thick bank of cloud. "We mustn't lose sight of it!" cries Tigerlily and orders the travel cloud forward. As they soar up after the peacock, the pair see the turrets of an imposing castle, surrounded by hundreds of birds. "Of course!" gasps Rupert. "It's heading for the Bird King's palace . . ."

RUPERT WITNESSES A ROW

The peacock's such a startling sight
That all the birds fly off in fright!

The pals land in the courtyard too –
"I wonder what the King will do?"

At least Bill's safe – he says he found
It thrilling once they left the ground!

The peacock cries out angrily –
Whatever can the matter be?

The peacock swoops down and lands in the courtyard of the great palace. All the birds are astonished to see Bill perched on its back, and fly off in alarm the moment the mysterious newcomer arrives. "We'll land in the courtyard too!" declares Tigerlily and orders the travel cloud to stop. "I hope the Bird King won't be too angry when he sees us," says Rupert. "He doesn't like strangers visiting his palace and hates the idea of anyone flying except birds . . .

As soon as the travel cloud lands, Rupert and Tigerlily hurry over to Bill, to make sure he's all right. "Yes, thanks!" he smiles. "The peacock's quite friendly, really. It landed gently to make sure I didn't fall off.' "Why has it come here?" asks Rupert. "I don't know," replies Bill, "but it seems to be having some sort of row . . ." As the pals turn round, they see the peacock arguing with one of the King's courtiers. "Oh, no!" cries Tigerlily. "He's summoning the guards!"

*A bird explains. "The Chamberlain
Has said your peacock can't come in!"*

*The Archivist brings out a book
Which tells how each bird's meant to look . . .*

*"It has no feathers! Our law's plain –
This leafy creature can't remain!"*

*The King appears. "Please let me stay!"
The peacock hurries up to say . . .*

"What's the matter?" Rupert asks a nearby bird. "The Chamberlain claims that the newcomer's an imposter!" it declares. "He's sent for the Royal archivist to prove that it cannot be a peacock, as it claims . . ." At that moment, a courtly looking bird appears carrying a large book. "Now we'll see!" announces the Chamberlain. "All types of bird are recorded in the King's guide. I'm sure there's nothing about green peacocks who have leaves instead of feathers . . ."

"As I thought!" declares the Chamberlain. "This leafy creature can't be a proper bird!" As he speaks, the King arrives and demands to know what's causing all the commotion. The peacock hurries forward and tells him how he's flown all the way from Nutwood to seek admission to the palace. "Please let me stay," it begs. The King looks thoughtful, then turns to Rupert and Tigerlily. "You are from Nutwood too," he says. "Tell me more about this strange bird . . ."

RUPERT COMFORTS THE PEACOCK

When Rupert tells him what's occurred
He says he can't admit the bird.

Defeated by the King's reply,
The peaock gives a mournful cry.

"Cheer up!" smiles Rupert. "Come with me!
Nutwood is where your home should be . . ."

"Quite right!" the King declares. "I'll call
Two eagles to escort you all."

The King listens gravely as Rupert tells how the peacock came to life, escaped from his garden, and finally flew off with Bill on its back. "I thought as much!" he says. "I'm afraid the Chamberlain is right. Although this strange creature *looks* like a bird, it cannot stay here, after all." When the peacock hears the King's words, it makes a low clucking sound and hangs its head sadly. "Poor thing!" says Tigerlily. "It seems such a shame . . ."

Rupert kneels down to talk to the dejected peacock. "Never mind," he says gently. "You can always come back to your old home in Nutwood. We all think you're very handsome. And besides, you'll be the only peacock in the whole village!" The peacock looks up, then starts to preen its leafy wings. "Will you come with us?" asks Tigerlily. "Yes," the peacock nods. "Bravo!" declares the King, and summons two of his swiftest eagles to lead the visitors.

RUPERT FLIES BACK

They bid the King farewell and then
Fly back to Nutwood once again . . .

The eagles show them where to go
Till Nutwood reappears below . . .

The Conjurer says he can tell
The bird's been transformed by a spell.

"You must be careful! Promise me
You'll use your wand more carefully . . ."

When everyone is ready, Tigerlily orders the travel cloud to rise, with Rupert and Bill perched safely aboard. "What a splendid way of flying!" cries the King. "Much better than those noisy machines you normally use . . ." The peacock gives a squawk of farewell, then flies off with the King's eagles guiding the way. Before long, Rupert spots Nutwood down below. "Let's see if my father has returned yet," says Tigerlily, steering the cloud down towards the pagoda . . .

The moment the peacock lands, an angry Conjurer strides into the garden. "So *this* is the strange bird all Nutwood's been talking about!" he declares. "Another of my daughter's mischievous spells, I presume . . ." "I'm sorry," says Tigerlily. "I didn't mean any harm . . ." "Magic should never be taken lightly!" says the Conjurer. "Luckily, all is well, but in future you must take more care." As he turns towards the peacock, his frown gives way to a broad smile . . .

RUPERT LEADS THE PEACOCK HOME

He smiles then asks the pals to show
Him where the peacock hedge should go . . .

"Sit still!" he tells the bird. "I'll try
To break the spell that made you fly . . ."

The air is filled with stars once more,
Then all is as it was before.

"Why, Mrs. Bear!" he smiles. "I feel
Your hedge could fly – it looks so real!"

"I must admit, it's a clever spell!" says the Conjurer. "No wonder everyone was so surprised . . ." He thinks for a moment, then tells Rupert to lead the way back to his garden. As the peacock runs along behind Rupert and Bill, it seems delighted to be returning home. "That's right!" smiles the Conjurer as it flutters up on to the hedge. "I want you to sit perfectly still, while *I* try to make a spell." Pointing his wand at the bird, he slowly starts to chant a rhyme . . .

For an instant the air is filled with shimmering stars, then the peacock returns to being part of the hedge. The next moment, Mrs. Bear appears and greets the visitors. "Hello," smiles the Conjurer. "Rupert was just telling me all about your new hedge and I had to come and see it for myself . . ." "It *is* rather good, isn't it?" says Mrs. Bear. "Very lifelike!" says the Conjurer, winking at Rupert. "Very lifelike indeed . . ."

THE END

RUPERT and

*Rupert has come on holiday
With his friend, Bill, to Rocky Bay.*

Rupert and Bill are on holiday together at Rocky Bay. "What shall we do now we've finished our sandcastle?" asks Rupert. "I know!" says Bill. "Let's have a game of catch!" Leaving Rupert's parents to snooze in their deckchairs, the pair set off along the beach, throwing the ball higher and higher as they go. "Steady on!" laughs Rupert as it sails over his head. "I'd have to be a grasshopper to jump that high."

WAIT HERE

LOS
PRO

the Beachcombers

They play catch, but Bill throws too high
The ball sails up into the sky . . .

As Rupert runs to fetch it he
Hears someone crying helplessly . . .

Rupert runs to fetch the ball. He bends down, then hears a strange noise . . . "It sounds like someone crying!" he murmurs. "What's the matter?" calls Bill, coming to see why Rupert's taking so long. "Listen!" whispers Rupert. "What do you make of that?" "Somebody crying!" gasps Bill. Rupert listens again, then points to the rocky cliffs. "It seems to be coming from inside one of those caves . . ."

"What's wrong?" asks Bill. Then he hears too.
"There's someone in that cave, but who?"

RUPERT DISCOVERS A MERMAID

Although it's dark, the pals decide
To find out who can be inside . . .

"A little girl!" gasps Bill. "But why
Is she so sad? What's made her cry?"

"A Mermaid!" blink the startled pair
As she spins round to see who's there.

"I've lost my mother's silver comb!
She'll be so cross when I get home . . ."

The two pals peer cautiously into the gloomy cave. "Can you see anything?" hisses Bill. "No," says Rupert. "It's too dark, but the crying seems to be coming from over there . . ." As the pair venture further into the cave their eyes grow used to the dark and they spot a shadowy figure, sitting on a rock. "It's a little girl!" gasps Bill. "Let's see if she needs any help," says Rupert. "She might have been exploring in here then slipped over and twisted her ankle."

As they draw level with the little girl, the chums gasp in amazement . . . "It's a Mermaid!" marvels Bill. "Goodness!" she cries and jumps up in surprise. "I'm sorry if we startled you," says Rupert, "but my friend and I have come to see what's wrong." "It's my silver mirror and comb!" sobs the Mermaid. "I left them lying by the water's edge, but when I came back to get them they'd disappeared! My mother will be furious! She only lent them to me, you see . . ."

"You're not to worry any more!
We'll make a search along the shore . . ."

The chums look everywhere but still
Can't find it. "Nothing here!" calls Bill.

"We'll leave a pile of stones to show
How far we've searched before we go . . ."

"Come on, you two! It's time for tea!"
Calls Rupert's mother anxiously.

"Don't worry!" says Rupert. "Bill and I will search the shore. Your comb and mirror can't be far away. Perhaps they've been carried along by a wave, or covered over by drifting sand." "Do you think so?" asks the Mermaid. "It's very kind of you to help . . ." The two pals set off along the beach, but can find no sign of the missing objects. "There's nothing here," calls Bill, peering into a rock pool. "I can't see them either," says Rupert. "But let's keep looking until it's teatime . . ."

No matter how carefully the pals search they still can't find the little Mermaid's mirror and comb. "I know!" says Rupert. "We'll leave a marker here to show how far we've got, then come back tomorrow for another look . . ." The moment he has finished piling up a heap of stones, the pair race off along the beach to join Rupert's parents. "*There* you are!" cries Mr. Bear. "I was just thinking I'd have to come and look for you . . ."

RUPERT SPOTS A STRANGER

Next morning Rupert leads the way
To where the chums were yesterday.

The stones have gone and it seems that
Somebody's raked the sand all flat . . .

"It must have been that boy! Let's see
If he knows where the comb could be . . ."

"Wait!" Rupert cries. "Before you go . . .
There's something that we'd like to know."

Next morning, the two chums hurry down to the beach as soon as they've finished breakfast. "Come on!" calls Rupert. "Let's start searching!" He sets off along the shore, but to his surprise, the piles of stones the pals left behind is nowhere to be seen . . . "I'm sure it was somewhere near here," says Bill. "So am I," agrees Rupert. "There's something else that's odd, too! Look at the way the sand is all flat. It looks as though someone's combed it with a giant rake . . ."

"I was right!" calls Rupert, excitedly. "Look over there – by those rocks!" "A boy with a rake!" gasps Bill. "But surely he can't have tidied the whole beach?" "I don't know," says Rupert. "If he *has* been raking the sand, then perhaps he's come across the missing mirror. Why don't we ask him and see?" The pals call out to the distant figure, but he doesn't seem to hear. "Wait!" calls Rupert. "We'd like to know . . ." This time the boy stops and looks up with a start.

RUPERT AND BILL FOLLOW A TRAIL

The moment that the stranger hears
He runs away and disappears.

"I wonder who he is? I'm sure
I've never seen him here before . . ."

The two chums search the beach and find
The boy has left a trail behind.

"He must be near, let's see if we
Can catch him unexpectedly . . ."

As soon as he sees the two chums, the boy races off towards the rocks as fast as he can . . . "Come back!" calls Rupert, but it's no use. By the time he and Bill reach the spot where he was standing, the boy has completely vanished. "How strange!" says Bill. "I don't think we frightened him. It looked more as if he didn't want to be seen. Do you think he lives at Rocky Bay?" "I wonder?" muses Rupert. "He might do, though I'm sure I've never seen him here before . . ."

Determined to ask the boy if he's seen the Mermaid's mirror, Rupert and Bill start searching the beach for clues to where he's gone. "Look!" cries Rupert. "There's a trail of footprints in the sand. Let"s follow them!" "Good idea!" agrees Bill. "But we'll go in different directions round this rock, so he can't give us the slip." "Quiet as you can!" whispers Rupert. "He may be hiding somewhere nearby . . ."

END OF PART 1

RUPERT
and the Beachcombers

They find the boy. "Don't be afraid!
"We're seeking something that's mislaid . . ."

"I see! So you're beachcombing too
My name is Tad. That's what I do!"

"We Beachcombers discover most
Things people lose along the coast."

"We take them to Lost Property.
Your comb might be there – follow me . . ."

As Rupert and Bill tiptoe round the giant rock, they soon spot the boy. "Hello," calls Rupert. "Don't be frightened. We only wanted to ask you a question . . ." The moment he hears what they want, the boy smiles and willingly agrees to help. "You've come to the right person," he declares. "My name's Tad. I'm an apprentice Beachcomber. We find *everything* that's been left on the beach. The only thing is, we're meant to stay out of sight. That's why I ran away!"

"Beachcomber?" asks Bill. "That's right," says Tad. "We rake the sand each morning, to keep it neat and tidy." "What about the Mermaid's mirror?" says Rupert. "Did anyone find it lying by the sea?" "You'd better come and ask at Lost Property," declares the boy. "If they did, that's where it will be by now . . ." Carrying his rake on his shoulder, he leads them along a narrow path through the rocks. "This way," he calls. "I'll take you there on my way back to Headquarters."

46

RUPERT SEES A GIANT SANDCASTLE

"This secret tunnel's how we reach
Our King's Headquarters from the beach!"

"Gosh!" Rupert blinks. "I'd no idea
That anything like this was here . . ."

"Look at that sandcastle!" Bill cries,
Unable to believe his eyes.

"It's where we live!" smiles Tad. "But you
Will find the place you want here too . . ."

To the pals' surprise, the path seems to be a dead end, with a mass of tangled branches blocking the way. "It's a secret tunnel!" Tad smiles, pushing the leaves aside. "Nobody except us Beachcombers knows the way through . . ." Rupert and Bill follow him down a dark, rocky tunnel. As they emerge into the sunlight, they both blink in astonishment at the extraordinary sight which lies ahead. "Amazing!" gasps Rupert. "And we never knew it was here . . ."

"A giant sand-castle!" cries Bill. "That's right!" laughs Tad. "We all live there, together with our King." When they reach the castle, Tad tells the chums to ask at Lost Property about the Mermaid's mirror. "I'm sorry I can't come with you," he says. "But I'm already late for morning assembly. You need to go that way, towards the far end of the beach. They don't get many visitors, but if you explain what you're looking for, they should be able to help."

RUPERT VISITS LOST PROPERTY

Before long, Bill and Rupert see
A small hut, marked 'Lost Property'.

They wait for ages, then decide
To see if anyone's inside . . .

The shutters open and out stares
A lobster. "Who's there?" it declares.

"Speak up! What's that you're looking for?
A comb left lying by the shore?"

Rupert and Bill set off along the beach until they come to a small kiosk. "This must be the place Tad meant," says Rupert. "But it looks as if it's closed." Painted on the shutters is a sign which reads, 'Please wait'. "That's all very well," declares Bill, "but what if there's nobody here?" After a while, he knocks on the shutters and a voice answers: "Be with you in a moment!" The chums hear lots of locks and bolts being undone, then the shutters slowly start to swing open . . .

As the kiosk opens, a cross-looking lobster appears, holding a brass ear trumpet. "Should have said you were waiting!" it declares. "Who are you and what do you want?" "My name's Rupert and this is Bill," says Rupert. "Ill?" says the lobster. "If your friend's ill, you ought to go to the doctor's you know, not the Lost Property office . . ." "Not ill," shouts Rupert. "Bill. His name's Bill! We've come to ask about a mirror and comb that were lost on the beach yesterday."

RUPERT IS ASKED SOME QUESTIONS

He reaches down a big red book.
"Lost yesterday? Let's have a look . . ."

"Yes, here it is. Found by the sea,
A Beachcomber brought it to me."

"To claim an object from the beach
You fill a form in. Here's one each . . ."

As soon as Rupert's finished, he
Checks all the details carefully . . .

"Lost yesterday?" asks the lobster. "Let's have a look in the log. Everything the Beachcombers find is written down there, you know. There's a note of *where* they found it, *when* they found it and who the owners were. Not that many ever come to claim anything . . ." Turning the pages of a big red book, he stops suddenly and starts to read aloud. "Silver mirror and comb found lying by the water's edge. Yesterday morning, 10 past six." "Hurray!" cries Rupert. "We've found them!"

"I'm afraid it's not as simple as that!" snaps the lobster. "You'll each have to fill in a form! Make sure you both write clearly!" he demands, handing each of the chums a pencil. "You'd be amazed at some people. Can't even write their own name!" "There!" says Rupert, when he's finished filling in all the details. "Now can we have the comb and mirror back, please?" "Not yet," replies the lobster. "Got to read your answers to see that everything's in order . . ."

RUPERT IS NOT ALLOWED IN

*"A **Mermaid's** comb! You should have said,"*
The Lobster cries, and shakes his head.

"King Neptune's subjects can't apply
To claim back things they've lost! Goodbye!"

The two chums hurry off to find
If they can change the Beach King's mind.

Stern castle guards keep strangers out.
"No visitors allowed!" they shout.

As he reads their forms, the lobster begins to shake his head. "A Mermaid!" he cries. "You didn't tell me the mirror belonged to a Mermaid!" "Yes," says Rupert. "She left it by the water's edge." "Fruits of the sea!" declares the lobster. "Anything from Neptune's kingdom is ours when it's left on the sand. That's the rule. Our King's very firm about it, I'm afraid. Nothing I can do!" "But surely," begins Bill. "No!" snaps the lobster and closes the shutters of his kiosk . . .

"Oh, dear!" sighs Bill. "If the lobster won't give us the mirror, what can we do now?" "Let's go and see the King himself!" says Rupert. "When he hears how upset the Mermaid is, he might agree to help . . ." As the chums near the castle, Rupert points towards the drawbridge. "We're in luck!" he cries. 'It's still open!' The pair race over the bridge, only to find themselves confronted by two stern-looking sentries! "Halt!" they cry. "No strangers may enter the castle!"

RUPERT AND BILL MEET THE KING

The chums are just about to go
When Rupert spots someone they know . . .

Tad smiles. "These are my friends, you see.
Please let them come inside, with me."

"The King's room's this way!" Tad declares
And hurries up a flight of stairs.

He greets the King and then requests
A special favour for his guests . . .

"We've come to see the King," Rupert tells the sentries. "Impossible!" they reply. "Only Beachcombers may enter the castle!" "Look!" cries Rupert suddenly. "There's somebody we know . . ." "It's Tad!" gasps Bill. "Hello!" calls the little Beachcomber. "Wasn't the lobster able to help?" When he hears what's wrong, Tad soon persuades the guards to let the two chums through. "They're my friends!" he smiles. "We'll go and see the King together!"

Following Tad across a central courtyard, Rupert and Bill find the sandcastle is even bigger than it seemed from outside. "This way!" he calls. "The King's chamber is right at the top of the castle. He likes to look out over the whole beach . . ." As soon as they reach the King's apartments, Tad hurries forward to introduce the chums. "Visitors from Rocky Bay, your Majesty. They've come to ask if you can grant a special request . . ."

RUPERT
and the Beachcombers

The King is furious to learn
What Rupert wants him to return . . .

"Impossible! I can't agree.
All treasure found belongs to me!"

"Request denied! Now, off you go!"
A guard declares. "The King said no!"

"Don't leave just yet," Tad tells the pair.
"There's one last chance left, over there . . ."

"A request!" says the King. "What sort of request?" "It's to do with something that was left by the water's edge . . ." explains Rupert. "Well?" asks the King. "A Mermaid's comb and mirror!" says Bill. "We asked at Lost Property, but the lobster wouldn't give them back!" "Quite right!" cries the King. "Anything left on the sand is mine. That's what Neptune and I agreed. We can't start making exceptions, you know. It's out of the question. Guards! Show them out!"

At the King's command, the guards escort Rupert and Bill out of the castle. "Off with you now!" orders one of the sentries. "If the King said no, then that's that!" "I suppose he's right," sighs Bill. "We'd better be getting back to Rocky Bay . . ." "Wait!" calls a voice. "It's Tad!" says Rupert. "He's running towards us!" "Don't go yet," says the Beachcomber. "There's still a way you might get the mirror back! Follow me, to where those guards are roping off part of the beach . . ."

RUPERT AND BILL BUILD A CASTLE

"It's Castle Day – when we all test
Our skills to see who builds the best . . ."

He thinks the pals should both join in –
"You name your own prize if you win!"

The first thing that they have to do
Is join the spade and bucket queue . . .

Then, piling up the sand, they plan
The finest castle that they can . . .

"Whatever's happening?" asks Rupert. "It's Sandcastle Day!" laughs Tad. "Each year, the King holds a competition to see who can build the best castle. The winner can choose anything he wants from the Lost Property office as his prize . . ." As the pals look on, a crowd of people come running out of the castle and hurry along the beach. "Nearly everyone takes part," explains Tad. "If you build a castle you can enter the competition too!"

Rupert and Bill hurry along the beach in the same direction as everyone else . . . The first thing they do is queue up for a bucket and spade, which the lobster supplies from his stores. "Plenty here!" he chuckles. "It's amazing how many we find!" As soon as they've collected their spades, the pals choose a good spot to build a castle, then set to work . . . "This is fun!" smiles Rupert. "We'll make something really special, so the King is bound to notice . . ."

RUPERT WINS THE COMPETITION

The pair soon set to with a will,
"We'll show these Beachcombers!" says Bill.

A trumpet sounds; the King draws near,
Who's castle's going to win this year?

"A splendid fort! Bravo!" he cries.
"The visitors have won first prize!"

"Now, tell me what you'd like! I see . . .
Oh, very well then, I agree!"

Everywhere the chums look, people are busily building sandcastles of all shapes and sizes. "Come on!" calls Rupert. "Let's make sure ours is the best!" The pair work together, as fast as they can, determined to build the castle higher and higher . . . "There!" gasps Bill, mopping his brow. "It's finished at last!" At that very moment, a herald blows his trumpet and the King appears. "Stop work now!" calls a guard. "It's time for His Majesty to judge the castles."

Everyone stands to attention as the King begins his inspection. "My word!" he cries when he sees the chums' castle. "This is splendid! I award you both first prize!" "Bravo!" cheers the crowd. "What would you like?" asks the King. "Cricket bats? windmills? gold coins?" "Actually," says Rupert, "what we'd really like is the little Mermaid's mirror and comb . . ." "Very well," smiles the King. "This time you've won them, fair and square!"

54

RUPERT CLAIMS HIS PRIZE

A messenger is sent to find
The comb the Mermaid left behind . . .

The King presents the prize they've won.
"You earned it, fair and square. Well done!"

It's time the pals were on their way –
Tad leads them back to Rocky Bay . . .

It isn't long before they reach
The Mermaid's cave, down by the beach.

A herald hurries to the Lost Property office and soon comes back, bearing the Mermaid's mirror and comb. "There!" declares the King, presenting them to Rupert and Bill. "Now we'll have a party to celebrate!" "Thank you, your Majesty," says Rupert, "but we really should be getting back to Rocky Bay." "I see," says the King. "In that case, young Tad here will show you the way. Well done with your castle. It really is most impressive!"

"Your plan worked!" laughs Rupert as Tad leads them back through the tunnel to Rocky Bay. "Yes," says the Beachcomber, "but only because you built such a splendid castle! The King couldn't believe it hadn't been made by one of us!" Hurrying along the beach until they reach the Mermaid's cave, Rupert and Bill tell Tad they're going to give the comb and mirror back. "I've never met a Mermaid!" he tells them. "They're rather shy of shore-dwellers!"

RUPERT RETURNS THE LOST MIRROR

The little Mermaid's thrilled they've found
Her comb and mirror – safe and sound!

"Tad found them really. He's the one
You ought to thank for all he's done . . ."

"We"ve got to go now, straightaway . . .
Goodbye, until another day . . ."

*"So **there** you are!" cries Mrs. Bear.*
"Beachcombing all day! What a pair!"

Inside the cave, the two chums find the little Mermaid sitting on a rock. "We've brought you these," says Rupert holding up a silver mirror. "Oh, thank you!" cries the Mermaid. "Wherever did you find them?" "*We* didn't," laughs Bill. "It's thanks to Tad that we got them back." "Tad?" asks the Mermaid. "Hello!" smiles the Beachcomber. "It was nothing, really. If I'd known whose they were I'd have returned them straight away!"

"Time for us to go now," says Rupert. "My parents might be getting worried." Waving goodbye to Tad and the little Mermaid, the two friends hurry back along the beach as fast as they can. "*There* you are!" cries Mrs. Bear, as she catches sight of the pals. "I've been looking for you everywhere. Whatever have you been up to?" "Oh, nothing, really," says Rupert. "We were only doing a spot of beachcombing . . ."

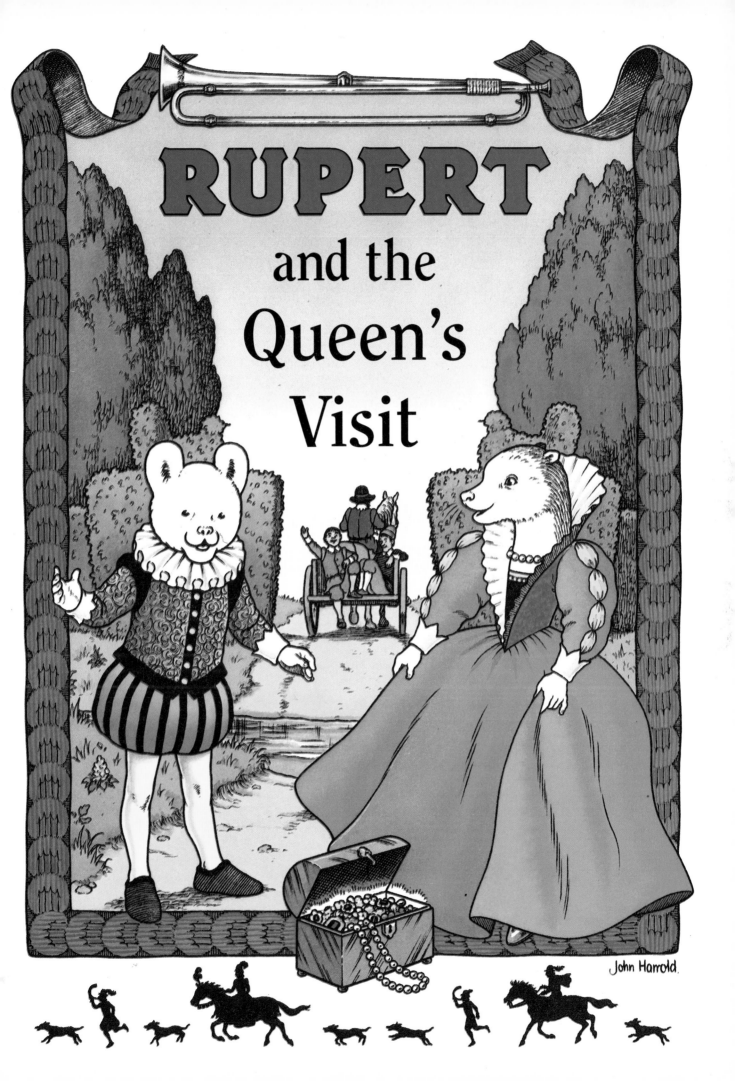

RUPERT
and the
Queen's
Visit

John Harrold.

RUPERT VISITS OTTOLINE

Rupert is on his way to see
His new friend, Ottoline, for tea.

"Hello!" she smiles. "How nice of you
To come and bring such nice flowers too!"

"I'll fetch a vase to put them in,
Says Mrs. Otter. "Do begin . . ."

The chums decide to look around.
"Come on! There's something new I've found . . ."

Rupert has been invited to tea by his new friend, Ottoline. Taking a bunch of flowers for Mrs. Otter, he sets off across the common towards Nutwood Manor . . . "I'm glad it isn't empty any more!" he thinks as he reaches the old house. "Before the Otters arrived, the grounds were so overgrown that you could hardly see the place." "Hello!" smiles Ottoline as she opens the door. "I'm ever so pleased you could come!"

While Rupert and Ottoline are enjoying their tea, Mrs. Otter arranges the flowers in a vase. "There!" she says. "They do look nice. I think I'll put them in the dining room . . ." As soon as the pair have finished, Ottoline tells Rupert that there is something she wants him to see. "I found it while I was exploring the house!" she explains. "There are so many rooms that I still haven't seen them all. This one's right at the top of the house, where nobody goes . . ."

RUPERT SEES A TAPESTRY

They walk towards a heavy door
That Rupert's never seen before . . .

His chum gestures excitedly
Towards a faded tapestry

"It shows how life here must have been
In olden days!" sighs Ottoline.

"The Queen and all her huntsmen stayed
In Nutwood, just as they're portrayed!"

"I wonder what Ottoline's found?" thinks Rupert. "Last time we went exploring, we came across a secret passage . . ." "This is the room!" declares Ottoline. "The door was jammed, but I managed to prise it open . . ." Following her inside, Rupert finds the room is completely empty. "Look over there!" says Ottoline, pointing at the far wall. "It's an old tapestry which shows how they used to go hunting. It must have been hanging here for hundreds of years . . ."

Moving nearer to the faded tapestry, Rupert sees an embroidered scene of two huntsmen blowing their horns, while a red-haired lady rides past on a splendid horse . . . "That's Queen Elizabeth!" sighs Ottoline. "She came to visit Nutwood once and stayed at the Manor, for a whole week. Imagine what it must have been like! Courtiers and musicians, huntsmen and servants, everyone waiting on the Queen. There was feasting and dancing every night!"

RUPERT'S PAL MAKES A WISH

"I wish that we could really see
The Royal Hunt, Rupert! You and me!"

The two friends hear a trumpet play
Then see two huntsmen ride away!

Next moment, they're amazed to find
They're in a forest of some kind . . .

"Incredible!" blinks Rupert. "I'm
Convinced that we've come back in time!"

"The Royal Hunt!" sighs Ottoline. "How I *wish* I could have seen it!" No sooner has she spoken, than Rupert hears the distant sound of dogs barking and a huntsman's horn, which grows louder and louder . . . "What's happening?" gasps Ottoline. The pair blink in astonishment as the tapestry seems to quiver and come to life. "They're moving!" cries Ottoline. "Look at the horses galloping through the trees! Everyone's trying to keep up with the Queen . . ."

"It all looks so life-like!" marvels Rupert. He turns round to look at the rest of the room, then cries out in disbelief . . . "Look! We're standing in the middle of a *real* forest!" The pair are completely dumbfounded. "H . . . how did we get here?" stammers Ottoline. "What's happened to the house? Where are we?" "I don't know," whispers Rupert. "There must be some kind of magic at work. The tapestry has come to life – and we've both become part of it . . ."

RUPERT GETS LOST

*The wood's so thick the pals don't know
Which way they ought to try to go . . .*

*"More huntsmen!" Rupert cries. "I say!
We're lost! Can you tell us the way?"*

*The men don't hear. Rupert calls, "Wait!
We need your help!" but it's too late . . .*

*Which way does Nutwood Manor lie?
The pals can't tell which path to try.*

Gazing anxiously at the thick forest which surrounds them, the two chums wonder what to do next . . . "If this is the same wood as the one in the tapestry, then Nutwood Manor can't be far away!" says Ottoline. The pair look all around, but there is no sign of any path. "Let's ask one of the huntsmen," says Rupert. He calls out as a horse gallops past, but the rider doesn't seem to hear. "Hello," he cries as a second man appears. "Can you tell us how to reach Nutwood Manor?"

To Rupert's dismay, the second rider doesn't seem to hear him either. "Wait!" call the pals as they run after the horsemen. But it's no use. The horses gallop ahead and have soon disappeared among the trees . . . "Which direction should we take now?" asks Ottoline. "I don't know," says Rupert. "That *may* be a path I can see over there, but the forest all looks the same after a while . . . "Let's try it," declares Ottoline.

61

RUPERT
and the Queen's Visit

They set off, but soon Rupert finds
The path they've chosen twists and winds . . .

The track runs out but then they hear
The sound of voices somewhere near.

"Three men!" says Ottoline. "They seem
To have got stuck, crossing the stream . . ."

"Hello there!" Rupert gives a call,
"Can we be any help at all?"

Rupert leads the way through the trees as the two pals set off along the winding path, which gets harder and harder to follow. Eventually, they reach the banks of a woodland stream. "It's a dead-end!" declares Rupert. "There's no sign of any path at all on the other side. I suppose we'll just have to turn round and go back the way we came . . ." "Wait," whispers Ottoline. "I'm sure I can hear voices. It's a group of people talking – and they're not very far away . . ."

Following the stream to where they can hear voices, Rupert and Ottoline come across three men, pushing a loaded cart along a muddy track. "Make haste!" calls the first, but the wagon seems stuck in the mud. "Zounds!" groans another. "We must quit Nutwood at once, before 'tis too late!" "Nutwood!" whispers Rupert. "We can't be far away . . ." Calling to the men, he steps forward and asks if they need help. "Thank you!" smiles their leader. "That *would* be kind . . ."

RUPERT HELPS THREE STRANGERS

The chums join in and help the three
To push their heavy wagon free . . .

Their leader thanks the chums and then
Says they'll be on their way again . . .

"We've come from yonder Manor where
We played for everybody there."

The three musicians wave goodbye.
"They're in a rush! I wonder why?"

Rupert and Ottoline begin to push the cart as hard as they can. At first nothing happens, then it slowly rolls clear of the mud. As they peer over the side, the pair notice that it is piled high with all kinds of musical instruments, which are perched on top of the men's load. "Well done!" cries their leader. "Without your help we would have been late for our next concert." "Concert?" asks Ottoline. "Yes," says the man. "We are a troupe of travelling musicians . . ."

The musicians explain that they are on their way from Nutwood, after a concert at the Manor. "That's where *we* want to go!" exclaims Ottoline. "Cross the stream and follow the path," declares the men's leader. "Nutwood Manor lies straight ahead . . ." The pair ford the stream, then wave farewell to their new friends. "Strolling players," sighs Ottoline. "I wonder where they're off to now?" "I wonder," says Rupert. "They seemed in a terrible hurry!"

RUPERT FINDS OTTOLINE'S HOUSE

"Unless the Queen's left Nutwood too
You'd think they'd stay here, wouldn't you!"

The pals keep going till they see
Smoke rising where the house must be . . .

"It's different now!" gasps Ottoline.
"Just like the pictures that I've seen . . ."

"Perhaps inside we'll find a way
To get back to the present day?"

"Fancy meeting someone who knows Nutwood Manor!" says Ottoline. "It's lucky they were able to show us the way . . ." "Yes," says Rupert. "But why were they leaving in the middle of the Queen's visit? I thought there was singing and dancing every evening of her stay." The pair continue along the path until they spot smoke rising from the chimney of a big house. "The Manor!" cries Ottoline. "I wonder if it looks very different? Let's go and see . . ."

Ottoline can hardly contain her excitement as the pals reach Nutwood Manor. "It *is* different!" she gasps. "Those tall hedges, are almost like a maze . . ." Nobody stirs as the pair hurry across the lawn. "I wonder what they'll make of us," whispers Ottoline. "I don't know," says Rupert as he rings the bell. "But I'm sure the house must hold the way back to our own time. We were upstairs when the tapestry came to life – perhaps the answer lies in the same room?"

RUPERT HEARS THE MAID'S TALE

The bell rings and a maid appears
But why is the poor girl in tears?

"Alas!" she sniffles. "Woe is me!
There's been a dreadful robbery . . ."

"The Queen went out and left behind
Her precious jewels for me to mind . . ."

"I checked the gems were safe, but then
They'd gone when I went back again!"

Although the pals hear a bell ring, it is a long time before anyone appears. At last, the door swings open and a young girl stands before them, with tears running down her cheeks. "Hello!" smiles Ottoline. "Is your mistress at home?" "No!" sniffs the girl. "They've all gone out hunting. I'm the only one here . . ." Dabbing her eyes with a handkerchief, she peers anxiously into the distance, towards the woods. "Whatever will they say when they get back?" she sobs.

"What's wrong?" asks Rupert. "Why are you so upset?" "The Queen's jewels!" exclaims the girl. "They were left behind for safe-keeping when everyone went hunting. I thought they were still in Her Majesty's room, but when I went to make sure, the whole casket had disappeared! The Queen will be furious when she finds out they've gone. Everybody's bound to say it's my fault. If only I had kept a more careful watch!"

END OF PART 2

RUPERT
and the Queen's Visit

Someone has robbed the Queen, but who?
"Three minstrels, who have vanished too!"

"Quick!" Rupert cries. "The men we met!
There might be time to stop them yet!"

The pals race back towards the ford.
"Their cart must have the jewels on board!"

The heavy wagon's tracks soon show
The chums which way they ought to go . . .

"Who can have taken the jewels?" asks Ottoline. "A group of rascally musicians!" declares the maid. "They waited until everyone had gone, then announced that they were leaving too. I didn't suspect them till after they had left, but I'm certain that's how the jewels came to disappear. They'd seen Her Majesty in all her finery the night before . . ." "The men we met!" cries Rupert. "There isn't a moment to lose . . ."

Leaving the maid to dry her eyes, Rupert and Ottoline run back through the forest, along the winding path. "We might just be in time!" calls Rupert as they reach the spot where they first met the three musicians and helped them free their cart. Crossing the ford, he peers closely at the ground, then gives a cry of triumph. "Look, Ottoline! Their cart is so heavily laden it has left a perfect set of tracks for us to follow. They can't be too far away, either . . ."

RUPERT FINDS THE THIEVES

The tracks stop, but then Rupert sees
A new trail in amongst the trees . . .

"They must be hiding somewhere near.
Yes! That's their voices I can hear!"

"We've caught them!" Rupert smiles. "But how
Can we get back the Queen's jewels now?"

An idea forms in Rupert's mind
"They've left their instruments behind . . ."

At first the tracks are easy to follow, but suddenly veer off into thick forest. "This way!" says Rupert. "I can see where the wagon has flattened the long grass . . ." "What do you suppose they're up to?" asks Ottoline. "That horse of theirs must be so exhausted they've decided to stop for a rest," suggests Rupert. "Besides, the woods are just the place to hide if you want to keep out of sight . . . Shush!" he whispers. "I can hear voices!"

Peering through a gap in the bushes, Rupert spots the three musicians, all gathered round a small box. Opening the lid, their leader pulls out a gleaming necklace and holds it up for the others to see. "Royal jewels!" he chuckles. "The finest in the land . . ." "We've caught them red-handed!" whispers Ottoline. "But how are we going to get the Queen's jewels back?" "I don't know," says Rupert. Then he catches sight of something on the musicians' wagon which gives him an idea . . .

RUPERT PLAYS A TRICK

He lifts a trumpet down and then
Goes back to Ottoline again . . .

"As soon as I begin to play,
Bark like a hound that's seen its prey!"

"Now!" Rupert calls. The pals begin –
As he blows, Ottoline joins in . . .

The three musicians hear the sound.
They drop the jewels and stare all round . . .

The musicians' wagon is still piled high with all their instruments. Rupert creeps towards it and seizes a strange-looking trumpet. Carrying it back to Ottoline, he quickly whispers the rest of his plan. "We'll try to trick the thieves," he explains. "As soon as I blow the trumpet, I want you to bark like a dog as loudly as you can." "All right!" agrees Ottoline. "But I don't see how it will help recover the jewels . . ." "Just watch!" smiles Rupert. "And don't stop till I say . . ."

Making sure that they are still well hidden by the bushes, Rupert and Ottoline get ready to try their plan . . . "Now!" nods Rupert and blows a long, loud note on the trumpet. Following his lead, Ottoline throws back her head and barks noisily like an excited hound . . . "Tis the Hunt!" cries the thieves' leader, dropping the casket in astonishment. "They must be coming this way!" "Quick!" calls a second robber. "Make haste before the Queen arrives. Every man for himself."

RUPERT RECOVERS THE JEWELS

Convinced the Hunt is on its way,
The thieves run off in disarray . . .

The two chums search until they find
The jewels the men have left behind.

The pair run off in case the men
Decide that they'll come back again . . .

Can they return the jewels in time,
Before the Queen learns of the crime?

Rupert keeps blowing the trumpet until he's quite sure the thieves have disappeared into the woods. "They've left the casket behind!" he calls to Ottoline. "Now's our chance . . ." Hurrying into the clearing, the pair scoop up the stolen jewels and put them carefully back in their case. "We certainly fooled those three!" laughs Ottoline. "Yes," smiles Rupert. "But they might decide to come back when they realise what's happened! Let's set off straightaway . . ."

Clutching the precious casket under his arm, Rupert leads the way back to Nutwood Manor. "Do you think they might follow us?" asks Ottoline anxiously. "Not once we're near the house!" says Rupert. "Even those three will know better than to show their faces there . . ." Hurrying the cart-tracks back the way they came, the pair reach the stream and bound across with a flying leap. "Not much further now!" calls Rupert. "I hope we're in time to help the maid!"

69

RUPERT SAVES THE DAY

"Well done!" the overjoyed maid cries,
Unable to believe her eyes . . .

Then, suddenly, the real Hunt comes,
Riding towards the startled chums.

"Quick!" calls the maid. "We'll go inside.
I'll show you somewhere you can hide . . ."

"The jewels are safe, but how will we
Make music for Her Majesty?"

When Rupert and Ottoline reach Nutwood Manor, the delighted maid can hardly believe her eyes. "The casket!" she cries. "But how did you manage to get it back?" Before he can explain, Rupert hears the sudden call of a *real* hunting horn. "Goodness!" gasps the maid. "The hunters must be on their way. I'll just have time to return Her Majesty's jewel case . . ." As she speaks, barking dogs run excitedly towards the house, and a group of stately riders comes into view.

Hurrying inside, the maid leads the pals straight to her room. "Wait here!" she says. "I'll be back in a few moments." When the maid returns, she is carrying a tray of food for Rupert and Ottoline. "You must be hungry!" she smiles. "Eat and drink your fill, then we'll decide what's to be done next." "At least you've seen the last of those musicians," declares Rupert. "Musicians!" gasps the maid. "I'd quite forgotten. Who's going to play at this evening's concert?"

RUPERT DRESSES UP

"I know!" says Ottoline. "I'll play!
At home I practice every day . . ."

The maid goes off to fetch the pair
Some special clothes they'll have to wear . . .

They put them on and both appear
As if they came from yesteryear . . .

She leads them to a gallery . . .
"The ball will start soon, wait and see . . ."

"I can play the piano!" says Ottoline. "Piano?" asks the maid. "What sort of instrument is that?" "Like this!" says Ottoline, pretending to play . . . "You mean a spinet!" laughs the maid. "We have one of those in the Minstrels' Gallery, if you really think you can manage . . ." Delighted at the thought of playing for Queen Elizabeth, Ottoline is even more thrilled when the maid fetches a beautiful dress for her to wear. "You'll have to dress up too!" she tells Rupert.

"Look at me!" cries Ottoline. "I've only ever seen dresses like this in old paintings. How wonderful to try one . . ." "I look like a painting too!" laughs Rupert. "It's just like fancy dress!" "This way!" calls the maid. Following her up a narrow staircase, Rupert and Ottoline find themselves in a long, thin room, where the spinet stands waiting, with the lid propped open. "Marvellous!" smiles Ottoline. "There's just time to practise before the guests arrive . . ."

RUPERT SEES THE QUEEN

"They're ready to start dancing now!"
Says Rupert as the men all bow.

Then everybody turns – the Queen!
"She's really here!" gasps Ottoline.

As Ottoline peers all around
Rupert can hear a knocking sound . . .

He hurries to the door, then blinks,
"Why's Mrs. Otter here?" he thinks . . .

As Ottoline plays the spinet, the ballroom down below slowly fills with a host of richly-dressed courtiers and noblemen. "They're ready!" declares Rupert. "I'll begin with a jig!" smiles Ottoline. "That should get everybody dancing . . ." As Rupert watches the swirling couples, the ballroom suddenly grows silent and everyone starts to bow. "The Queen!" gasps Ottoline. "Doesn't she look splendid? She's wearing all the jewels we rescued!"

"She's greeting each of her courtiers in turn," says Ottoline, peering excitedly at the Queen. "I expect they're talking about the day's hunting. As soon as they've finished I'll play another tune." To Rupert's surprise, he suddenly hears a knocking sound, which grows louder and louder. "There's somebody at the door," he thinks and hurries to see who's there. The door swings open and Ottoline's mother appears! "There you are," she smiles. "I couldn't think where you'd got to . . ."

RUPERT'S ADVENTURE ENDS

"Quick, come and see the dancers too!"
"Dancers?" she smiles. "There's only you . . ."

The chums peer down and find that they
Have come back to the present day . . .

"The tapestry!" gasps Ottoline.
"We went inside and met the Queen!"

"The Queen!" her mother gasps. "Bless me!
You'll have to tell me, over tea . . ."

"Come and look at the dancers," cries Ottoline as her mother steps into the room. "Where?" asks Mrs. Otter. "There's nothing here except that old tapestry." "Tapestry?" blinks Rupert. "Of course! It all came to life . . ." Looking down, the pals see that their finery has vanished and they are back in their normal clothes. "W . . . what happened?" gasps Ottoline. "The Queen was here, with all her courtiers. Or rather, we were there . . ." "Where?" asks Mrs. Otter.

"Inside the tapestry!" declares Ottoline. "Rupert and I heard dogs barking and the next moment we saw Queen Elizabeth come riding past with all the hunters . . ." "Queen Elizabeth?" blinks Mrs. Otter. "Yes!" says Rupert. "We saved her jewels from robbers. Then Ottoline played the spinet . . ." "Goodness!" smiles Mrs. Otter. "Come and have some tea while you tell me all about it . . ."

THE END

RUPERT

*"Look, Rupert! Special post today –
This letter's come a long, long way . . ."*

Early one morning, Rupert and his parents hear a knock at the front door. "It's the postman!" cries Rupert and hurries to see what he's brought. "Special letter from overseas!" declares the postman. "Looks like it's come a long way . . ." "Goodness!" exclaims Mr. Bear. "It's from Uncle Boris. He wants us to go and visit him – in Russia!" "Can we?" asks Rupert excitedly. "Yes," smiles his father. "We could do with a change of scene!"

and Uncle Boris

"From Russia!" exclaims Mr. Bear.
"Uncle Boris invites us there!"

"We'll pack warm clothes, in case there's snow,"
Says Mrs. Bear. "You never know . . ."

"To think we're going all that way!" says Mrs. Bear as she helps Rupert pack his case. "I've always wanted to see Russia . . ." "What's it like?" asks Rupert. "Cold!" says his mother. "That's why we're taking plenty of warm clothes." When everything is ready, Mr. Bear loads the cases into the car and sets off for the coast. "Goodbye!" calls Rupert, waving to his chums. "I'll send you a postcard as soon as we arrive!"

At last the journey has begun.
"Goodbye!" call Rupert's pals. "Have fun!"

RUPERT GOES ON A JOURNEY

They reach the coast, then climb aboard
A ship that's due to sail abroad.

"Is that Russia?" asks Rupert. "No!"
Laughs Mr. Bear. "We've miles to go . . ."

"We've just reached France now," he explains.
"From here we'll catch one of these trains."

The train has beds inside so they
Can sleep while speeding on their way . . .

When they reach the coast, Mr. Bear leads the way to a large ship waiting by the quay-side. "This is the next stage of the journey!" he tells Rupert as they climb the gangplank and join the other passengers. When everyone is safely aboard, the ship's horn sounds and they set sail. For a long time all Rupert can see is water on every side, but, suddenly, he catches sight of land. "Is that Russia?" he asks. "No!" laughs his father. "We've got a long way to go yet . . ."

"We're in France now, Rupert!" says Mrs. Bear. Hailing a taxi, they soon arrive at a busy station where people are all hurrying to catch their trains. "This is ours!" says Rupert's father. "The Super-Express . . ." The train is the biggest that Rupert has ever seen and has a splendid dining car, where the Bears have supper. At the end of the meal they are shown to a special carriage. "It's a sleeper," explains Mr. Bear. "We'll be travelling all through the night . . ."

RUPERT MEETS UNCLE BORIS

Next morning, when they look outside,
The Bears see Russian countryside . . .

The train stops and they clamber out –
But hardly anyone's about . . .

Then Uncle Boris gives a call.
"Hello!" he cries and hugs them all.

"Now, Little Nephew! Come with me!
There's so much here for you to see . . ."

Next morning, Rupert looks out of the window and spots a strange looking spire. "We must have arrived in Russia!" declares Mr. Bear. Studying his guidebook carefully, he announces that they should soon be reaching Uncle Boris's village. The train stops and they get out at a tiny station with hardly anyone there. "I hope this is the right place," says Mrs. Bear anxiously. "Yes!" says Rupert. "Look! That must be Uncle Boris waiting for us, over there."

"Tovarish!" cries Uncle Boris, hurrying to greet Rupert's father. "How marvellous that you managed to come! Your wife is even prettier than I imagined and this – why, this must be little Rupert." Reaching out to shake his Uncle's hand, Rupert finds himself lifted high in the air and perched on Boris's shoulder. "Come!" he declares, picking up the cases as if they weighed nothing. "We'll set off straightaway . . ."

END OF
PART
1

RUPERT
and Uncle Boris

*"We'll travel in this horse-drawn cart.
I'll load your things in, then we'll start!"*

*Boris explains his cottage lies
Within a forest of great size.*

*Their way grows gloomy as they go
Through thick woods where tall fir trees grow . . .*

*Then, in the darkness, Rupert sees
A golden bird fly through the trees!*

Uncle Boris leads the way to a heavy, horse-drawn cart. "Not very luxurious!" he declares, "but there'll be plenty of room if Rupert travels in the back . . ." Rupert clambers into the straw-filled wagon and is soon peering excitedly at the tall trees which surround them on every side. "A Russian forest!" says Mrs. Bear. "Yes," laughs Boris. "But this is only the edge! Our forests are so big, you can walk through them for days without meeting another soul . . ."

As they journey on through the towering trees, the forest looks darker and darker, as if the sun never penetrates its silent gloom. Suddenly, Rupert spots a light moving in amongst the branches of the trees. "I wonder what it could be?" he thinks to himself. As the wagon draws nearer, he's astonished to see a strange bird, with feathers that sparkle and shimmer . . . "Look!" he calls excitedly, but, by the time the others have turned to see, the bird has disappeared . . .

RUPERT HEARS ABOUT THE FIREBIRD

When Boris hears what Rupert saw
He smiles. "It's the Firebird! I'm sure . . ."

Before long, they complete their ride.
"I'll tell you more when we're inside . . ."

"But first of all we need a cup
Of Russian tea to warm us up!"

"To see the Firebird's very rare!
Most people never know it's there . . ."

"What was it?" asks Uncle Boris. "Some sort of bird!" gasps Rupert. "Its feathers were glowing in the dark . . . "That sounds like the Firebird!" exclaims his uncle. "Firebird?" asks Rupert. "I'll tell you about it later," says Boris. "We're nearly then now. That's my house you can see, in the clearing." Ahead of them stands a large wooden cabin with a thatched roof. "Plenty of time for story-telling later!" laughs Boris. "The first thing we need is some nice hot tea . . ."

"Sweet, black tea from a samovar!" smiles Uncle Boris. "There's nothing quite like it after a long ride through the forest . . ." "What about the Firebird?" asks Rupert. "It's a Russian legend," explains his uncle. "The stories say it flies through the forest, lighting its way with feathers that glow like fire . . ." "That's what I saw!" cries Rupert. "Then you are very fortunate!" answers Boris. "The bird is so rare that many say it can't exist."

RUPERT LEARNS A NEW DANCE

*The Rupert's uncle sings of when
It led a lost boy home again.*

*"Its glowing feathers lit the way –
The darkness was as bright as day!"*

*"Let's have some Russian dancing now!
Come on, Nephew! I'll show you how . . ."*

*As Boris dances, Rupert tries
To join in too. "What fun!" he cries.*

As Rupert's parents finish drinking their tea, Uncle Boris produces a balalaika and starts to strum it thoughtfully . . . To Rupert's delight, he begins to sing, all about a young woodcutter, who got lost in the forest and called to the Firebird to show him how to get home. "And it did?" asks Mrs. Bear. "Of course!" smiles Uncle Boris. "It's a happy song. The bird lit the way, the young man returned to his village and, for all I know, he's probably living there still . . ."

After he's finished the Firebird song, Uncle Boris plays some more tunes on his balalaika, then tells Rupert he'll teach him how to do a Russian dance . . . "Just follow me!" he laughs, springing from one foot to the other, as Mr. and Mrs. Bear clap to keep time. "Bravo!" he calls as Rupert joins in. "You dance just like a little Russian! Now you'll really have something to show your friends back in England. You'll be the only Russian dancer in the whole of Nutwood . . ."

RUPERT JOINS HIS UNCLE

The dancing ends – a feast begins.
"We'll celebrate now!" Boris grins.

Then soon it's time to say goodnight,
"Tomorrow we'll explore! Sleep tight!"

Next morning Rupert's woken by
The bright sun in a cloudless sky . . .

His uncle's awake early too –
"Can I come mushrooming with you?"

"Phew!" puffs Uncle Boris. "All that singing and dancing has made me hungry!" Disappearing into the kitchen, he comes back with a steaming dish of food. "A special feast to celebrate your arrival . . ." After all the adventures of the day, Rupert is feeling very sleepy. "Come on!" smiles Mrs. Bear, as soon as dinner is over. "Time you were in bed!" "This way," says Boris. "Sleep well, Little Nephew. Tomorrow we'll explore the forest . . ."

Next morning, Rupert is woken up by a shaft of brilliant sunshine. "W . . . where am I?" he blinks, then smiles as he suddenly remembers. "Russia!" Inside the cabin everything is so quiet that Rupert thinks he must be the only one awake. Opening the door, he's surprised to find Uncle Boris setting out with an empty basket. "Hello!" he cries. "I'm just off to pick a few mushrooms for breakfast." "Can I come too?" asks Rupert. "Of course!" laughs Boris.

The pair start searching near the trees –
"Make sure that they all look like these!"

Soon Rupert spots a clearing where
More mushrooms grow. "I'll try in there . . ."

He picks the mushrooms, then spots more.
"They're just the same as these, I'm sure!"

It's only when Rupert turns back
He sees he's wandered off the track!

"Gathering mushrooms is a favourite Russian pastime," says Uncle Boris as the pair set off into the woods. "It's easy when you know what to look for – stick to ones like this and be careful not to pick any toadstools!" As soon as they reach a clearing in the trees, Boris spots a clump of mushrooms and starts to fill his basket. "There are some more just behind that tangle of bushes," thinks Rupert. "If I slip through the gap I'm sure I'll be able to reach them . . ."

To Rupert's delight, he finds a grassy clearing, where lots of mushrooms grow. As soon as he's picked the first few, he spots another cluster, then a third that he can't resist gathering too. Only when his basket is almost full does Rupert think of going back to join his uncle. "Now, which way did I come?" he thinks. As he looks all round, he suddenly realises how far he's wandered into the forest. "Oh dear! It all looks the same . . ."

END OF PART 2

These two pictures of Rupert and Rika look identical, but there are ten differences between them. Can you spot them all? *Answers on page 93.*

PART 3

RUPERT
and Uncle Boris

He calls his uncle – no reply!
There's no-one there to hear his cry . . .

"Which way?" he thinks. "I just can't see
The path. I know! I'll climb this tree . . ."

He clambers up and doesn't stop
Until, at last, he nears the top.

"I've made it!" Rupert gasps. "Oh, no!
*I **still** can't see which way to go . . ."*

Realising that he's lost in the forest, Rupert calls to his uncle as loudly as he can. "Help!" he cries. "Uncle Boris! Can you hear me?" As he listens for a reply, all Rupert can hear is the sound of his own voice echoing through the trees. "He must be too far away . . ." he thinks. "Whatever shall I do?" Sitting down to gather his thoughts, he suddenly has a good idea. "I'll climb to the top of one of these trees! With a bit of luck I should be able to see the roof of the cabin . . ."

Clambering up through the branches of the tree, Rupert keeps listening for his uncle's voice. "Perhaps he's still looking for me?" he thinks. "I hope my parents won't be too worried when they hear what has happened. I'm bound to find them, sooner or later . . ." When he reaches the top of the tree, Rupert pushes his way through a canopy of leaves, only to find himself surrounded by dense forest on every side. "Oh, no!" he groans. "I still can't see any sign of the cabin at all!"

RUPERT FINDS THE FIREBIRD

Then, down below, a light appears.
"There's somebody nearby!" he cheers.

He scrambles quickly to the ground
And runs towards the light he's found.

As Rupert nears the shining light
He wonders what can be so bright . . .

"The Firebird! But it's locked inside
A cage, to which a rope's been tied!"

Unable to spot his uncle's cabin, Rupert is about to climb back down again when he suddenly notices a light flickering in the depths of the forest. "There must be somebody down there!" he thinks. "If I hurry, they might be able to tell me how to find the right path . . ." Scrambling down the tree, Rupert picks up his basket and runs towards the light, which he can still see, glinting through the gloom. "Wait!" he calls breathlessly. "Don't go off without me . . ."

As Rupert hurries through the forest, the flickering light grows brighter and brighter. "I must be getting near!" he thinks. "Perhaps it's somebody's camp?" The glow seems to be coming from a small clearing in the trees. The moment Rupert reaches it he gasps in amazement, for hanging from the branch of a tree is a strange looking bird locked in a sturdy cage. "The Firebird!" Rupert cries. "So that's what I could see glowing in the dark!"

RUPERT IS CAPTURED

The moment Rupert comes in sight
The Firebird squawks with all its might . . .

"Don't be afraid!" he starts to call,
Then suddenly hears something fall . . .

A net! Now Rupert's been caught too!
Someone has trapped them both – but who?

"You thief!" an angry stranger cries.
"Admit you"ve come to steal my prize!"

Still marvelling at his strange discovery, Rupert steps into the clearing to take a closer look at the firebird, whose feathers sparkle and shimmer like glowing coals. The moment it sees him, the bird squawks in alarm and starts to flap its wings wildly. "Please don't be frightened," says Rupert. "I didn't mean to startle you . . ." As he reaches the cage, Rupert suddenly hears an odd swishing sound high above his head. "W . . . what's happening?" he gasps. "Who's there?"

A net! Before Rupert can move, he finds himself trapped under a heavy net, which knocks him to the ground. Struggling to his feet, he sees a tall figure, glaring angrily down at him. "So! You have come to steal the Firebird," cries the man. "No," gasps Rupert, but his captor takes no notice. "I might have known that someone would try to take my prize!" he growls. "It's as well that I laid a trap to capture all who tried. You were looking at the bird's cage, weren't you?"

RUPERT MEETS A HUNTER

"No!" Rupert says. "I'm lost, you see.
The bright light's what attracted me . . ."

"Lost?" smiles the man. "I think I know
The very way you ought to go!"

The pair set off without delay,
"Your uncle's cabin lies this way . . ."

"My camp's in this direction too.
Let's stop for lunch. I've made a stew!"

"I wasn't trying to steal the Firebird!" protests Rupert. "I got lost in the forest and saw its feathers glowing in the dark . . ." "Lost?" says the man. "And what were you doing here in the woods?" "Picking mushrooms," explains Rupert. "I wandered off the path and couldn't find the way to my uncle's cabin." "You should be more careful!" warns the man. "The forest is probably full of thieves, all looking for a prize like mine. Not to worry! I'll show you the way to go . . ."

Untying the cage from the tree, the man sets off through the forest with the Firebird still safely inside. "This way!" he declares. "Luckily, I know exactly where your uncle lives . . ." As Rupert follows, the path twists and turns then suddenly ends in a small clearing. "W . . . where are we?" blinks Rupert. "My camp!" smiles the man. "It's on the way to your uncle's, so I thought we'd stop for some lunch. It won't take long," he adds. "Everything should be ready by now . . ."

RUPERT GETS A WARNING

"Eat all you like!" the stranger smiles.
"You must have walked for miles and miles!"

The man nods off and Rupert yawns –
"Don't fall asleep!" the Firebird warns.

"The hunter means to catch you too
And sell us to a far-off zoo!"

The bird tells Rupert, "Take the key
That's on his belt and set me free . . ."

In no time at all, Rupert is sitting down to a delicious plate of stew . . . "Nothing like it after a morning's hunting!" laughs the man. "I mean, hiking! Hiking through the woods . . ." As soon as they've finished lunch, he settles down for a nap. "Won't be long!" he yawns. "Just forty winks, then we'll go . . ." Feeling drowsy after the long walk, Rupert closes his eyes and soon starts to fall asleep too. "Wake up!" cries the Firebird suddenly. "Wake up, little bear . . ."

"Beware!" squawks the Firebird. "You are in terrible danger! The hunter is not as friendly as he seems, but has been leading you further and further from your uncle's cabin. He means to trick you and sell us both to the circus in St. Petersburg!" "W . . . what shall I do?" gasps Rupert. "Release me from this cage!" cries the bird. "All you need is the little key he keeps tied to his belt. Take it while he's still fast asleep and I promise you, all will be well . . ."

RUPERT UNLOCKS THE CAGE

He reaches for the key, but then
The man starts to wake up again!

He stirs but doesn't feel a thing
As Rupert gently tugs the string . . .

"Well done!" the Firebird calls. "Now try
To let me out, so I can fly . . ."

The cage unlocks. "Good!" smiles the bird.
"I don't think that the hunter's heard . . ."

Hardly daring to breathe, Rupert tip-toes silently towards the sleeping figure. He can see the key, hanging from a loop of string, and decides to untie it straight away . . . As he reaches out, the hunter starts to stir, then gives a mighty yawn! "Oh, no!" thinks Rupert. "He mustn't wake up yet . . ." Luckily, the man rolls over and begins to snore, louder than ever. The moment Rupert's sure he's fast asleep, he unties the string and gently removes the key . . .

Slipping the key safely into his pocket, Rupert begins to clamber up the tree, towards the bird's cage. "Well done!" it whispers. "Now you can set me free . . ." As soon as Rupert reaches the cage, he takes the key and turns it in the lock. To his dismay, nothing happens – it must be the wrong one! "Try again!" hisses the Firebird. This time it turns with a sharp click and the padlock springs open. "Excellent!" smiles the bird. "Now we can *both* escape . . ."

RUPERT RELEASES THE FIREBIRD

It flaps its wings and squeezes out –
The hunter gives a startled shout . . .

"Come back!" he calls in fury. "Wait!"
But off the bird flies. It's too late!

And then, before the hunter sees,
Rupert shins down the tree and flees . . .

The Firebird joins him. "Now I'll show
The proper way you need to go."

While Rupert watches from the branches of the tree, the Firebird squeezes through the cage door and takes off with a ruffle of feathers. At the sound of its wings, the hunter wakes with a start, then springs to his feet. "Come back!" he cries, waving his arms wildly, but it's too late . . . The bird circles higher and higher, then soars away over the tree tops. "Oh, no!" thinks Rupert. "It's flown off and left me! How can I find my way back to Uncle Boris's cabin now?"

Dismayed at the loss of his prize, the hunter hurries away in pursuit of the Firebird . . . As soon as he has gone, Rupert slides down the tree and runs off in the opposite direction. "I don't know where I'm going, but at least I'm free!" he thinks. Pushing his way through the trees, he suddenly spots a glimmer of light and finds the Firebird, pointing the way. "Follow me!" it cries. "Now I've thrown the hunter off the scent, I'll take you back to your uncle . . ."

RUPERT IS LED SAFELY HOME

The bird flies on and lights the track
For Rupert as they hurry back.

"We're nearly there! Just follow me
Towards the smoke that you can see . . ."

At last the cabin comes in view
"I'm home!" cries Rupert. "Thanks to you!"

"Thank goodness!" Uncle Boris cheers –
At once the Firebird disappears . . .

With the Firebird flying on ahead to light the way, Rupert follows a winding path through the gloomy forest. "No wonder it's so easy to get lost!" he thinks. "If it wasn't for the glow of the bird's feathers, I'd *never* find the way . . ." After a long journey through the thickest part of the forest, Rupert suddenly spots a plume of smoke, rising high into the air. "A chimney!" he cries. "That's right!" calls the Firebird. "Your uncle's cabin lies just beyond those tall trees . . ."

Soon Rupert finds himself at the edge of a familiar clearing. "Hurray!" he cries. "There's Uncle Boris's cabin!" "I told you I'd find it!" laughs the bird. "You'd better hurry back now and let them know you're safe . . ." Rupert's uncle is overjoyed to see him. "Thank goodness!" he cries. "I looked everywhere I could think of, but you seemed to have disappeared." "The Firebird led me back," says Rupert. He looks round, but the bird has disappeared . . .

RUPERT BIDS THE BIRD FAREWELL

*When Rupert's parents hear he's found
They're overjoyed he's safe and sound . . .*

*"The Firebird showed me where to go!
Its feathers really shine, you know!"*

*That evening, Rupert thinks he sees
A bright light high above the trees . . .*

*"The Firebird!" Uncle Boris cries.
Unable to believe his eyes . . .*

Rupert's parents are delighted to see that he's safe and sound. "Wherever have you been?" asks Mr. Bear. "Lost in the woods!" says Rupert. "I wandered off the path . . ." "You must be more careful!" warns Uncle Boris. "The forest can be a dangerous place! Now, come and have something to eat, and tell us all about the Firebird . . ." "It really did show me the way!" says Rupert as he recounts his adventure. "Its feathers lit the path, just like a glowing lantern . . ."

Later that evening, as Rupert gets ready for bed, he notices a shimmering light in the treetops outside. "The Firebird!" he cries excitedly. Everyone hurries outside to see as the bird swoops down towards the cabin, then flies off into the forest. "Goodbye!" calls Rupert. "Thanks for guiding me!" "Astounding!" gasps Uncle Boris. "I've seen the Firebird at last, and all because of you, Little Nephew!"

THE END

Follow **Rupert** every day

in the **Daily Express**

John Harrold.

ANSWERS TO PUZZLE: **Spot the Difference**
1. Light switch missing; 2. Door knob missing; 3. Pocket missing Rupert's coat; 4. Buttons missing Rupert's sleeve; 5. Cushion missing from chair; 6. Mr. Bear's pullover missing; 7. Middle button missing Mr. Bear's jacket; 8. Black stripe missing Rika's sleeve; 9. Drawer handle missing; 10. Slat missing from back of chair.

93